FOURTH GENERATION OF BODOLAND MOVEMENT: THE ROLE OF BONSU AND AIBPNLBS

RAJYA BIHIN RAJKUMAR

Contents

CHAPTER I

Introduction

The Bodos who are first settlers of Assam have been demanding a separate state to be created out of Assam since the late sixties. Mechanisms for this separate state demand changed from a democratic one to a violent upheaval at different points of time. Plains Tribals Council of Assam (PTCA) formed in 1967 not only taught the Bodos political consciousness but also a sense of having a separate homeland for the plains tribes of Assam. This party demanded a separate state named Udayachal in northern bank of mighty river Brahmaputra in Assam. Apart from the Bodos who constitute the largest plains tribe in Assam, this demand for Udayachal was supported by other plains tribes as it strove for inclusiveness. However, PTCA failed to fulfil its dream for Udayachal. The All Bodo Students' Union (ABSU) also formed in 1967 started withdrawing its support to the PTCA sometime in 1979. The fallouts of it were dangerous including the deadly fratricidal killings amongst the Bodos, destruction of livelihoods and burning of villages. This incident stands out as a the most tragic for the Bodos. PTCA became dormant after ABSU withdrew its support. Therefore, ABSU under the leadership of Bodofa Upendra Nath Brahma launched the movement for a full-fledged state of Bodoland in 1987.

Meanwhile, a militant outfit, the Bodo Security Force (BSF) was formed in 1986. It was rechristened as National Democratic Front of Bodoland (NDFB) in 1994. This outfit adopted violence as way to achieve its goal of creating a sovereign Bodo nation.

The first bipartite Bodo peace accord was signed in 1993 under the banner of ABSU and Bodo Peoples' Action Committee (BPAC) with Assam Government in presence of the then Union Minister Rajesh Pilot according a Bodoland Autonomous Council (BAC). It, however, miserably failed to fulfil the political aspirations of the Bodos. NDFB rejected this peace deal and its package. Hence they remained adamant at fighting for a sovereign Bodo nation. The failure of BAC was too poisonous as it paved the way for forming another militant outfit Bodo Liberation Tigers Force (BLT) in 1996 to fight for a separate state Bodoland within Union of India under the provision of the Constitution of India. Aftermath of BLT formation, the Bodos again entangled in ugly fratricidal killings.

However, after the short stint of violence, BLT signed the tripartite second Bodo peace accord with Government of India (GoI) and Assam Government in 2003 according the Bodoland Territorial Council (BTC)-an administrative entity created under the provision of Sixth Schedule of the Constitution of India. But this second peace treaty was also a failure as it couldn't serve the political aspirations of the Bodos. These two peace accords were only temporary measures to shun violence and bring an end to armed conflict in Bodo areas. The Bodos again vowed for separate state of Bodoland under the leadership of ABSU. NDFB remained as armed outfit indulging in violence across the state. Hence the second peace treaty also stood as sub-optimal.

NDFB vowed for full fledged separate state after it gave up the concept of sovereign Bodo nation after it came to a ceasefire agreement with GoI in 2005. In the long journey of armed conflict, it got split into four factions. NDFB (S) led by B. Saoraigwra which signed a ceasefire agreement with GoI a fortnight ago from its base in Myanmar. After its coming into ceasefire agreement, the tripartite third Bodo peace accord was signed on January 27, 2020. All the factions of NDFB, ABSU and UBPO (United Bodo People's Organisation) signed this new accord with GoI and Assam Government which is called the final and comprehensive peace deal with Bodo organizations demanding a separate state. This peace accord would bring to an end the final phase of Bodo militancy in Assam.

The outcome of this third accord is the creation of the Bodoland Territorial Region (BTR) without affecting the territorial integrity of Assam. It would have legislative, executive, administrative and financial powers on several policy areas. This new Bodoland would resolve for protection and development of language, art, culture, education and economy in the region. It is not a separate state but a state of Bodoland within the state of Assam. Despite being hailed as a historic Bodo peace accord, several pertinent questions are being asked. Would this peace accord bring permanent solution to the Bodo issues? Would demand for separate state of Bodoland come to an end? Would it serve the political aspirations of the Bodos? Would this new Bodoland deliver development to each and every person in the new dispensation?

This historic accord in the history of Bodoland movement would definitely bring the end of over 34 years of Bodo militancy in Assam. Both Central and State governments should expedite the implementation of clauses of accord in letter and spirit. Leaders, in the corridors of power, should know the purposes of creation of this new Bodoland. It is created by sacrificing many souls! All the people therein be they Bodos or non-Bodos

ought to get the privileges and share of the development
cake.

CHAPTER II

Role of Bodo National Students' Union (BoNSU)

A students' organisation has revived the Bodoland statehood demand in Assam amidst the BJP's claim of resolving the Bodo problem through the signing of the historic Bodoland Territorial Region (BTR) pact.

In a memorandum submitted to Prime Minister Narendra Modi through the Kokrajhar district magistrate, the newly-formed Bodo National Students' Union (BoNSU) said the Centre had, over the past 30 years, signed three peace accords with the Bodo leadership but failed to fulfil the aspirations of Bodos.

The students' body lamented that although the Bodos had struggled for long, their demands for socio-political, socio-cultural and economic development continued to remain unfulfilled.

BoNSU has stated that the Bodos' struggle for right to self-determination has its genesis in the British rule.

As early as the 1930s, GurudevKalicharan Brahma, the then lone leader of the Bodos, had submitted a memorandum to the Simon Commission demanding a political setup for the indigenous and tribal people of Assam. However, his demand for political administration was ignored by the British Raj. Even in the post-independence era, such demands were not met by successive governments.

In 1967, the Bodos had demanded the creation of a Union Territory "Udayachal", by carving out an area of

Assam from Sankosh to Sadiya along the foothills of Himalaya (Bhutan and Arunachal Pradesh), following the realisation that tribal blocks and belts notified by the British were being acquired by rich immigrant landlords.

Later in the 1980s, the All Bodo Students' Union (ABSU) had launched a mass movement. Almost around the same time, a section of the Bodo youth had taken up arms and formed an insurgent group, disillusioned by the government's apathy towards the Bodo movement.

Even as the struggle continued, the Assam government had formed the Bodoland Autonomous Council but the Bodos said it had failed to fulfil their socio-economic aspirations. Another accord, signed with insurgent group Bodo Liberation Tigers in 2003, had led to the creation of the autonomous Bodoland Territorial Council (BTC) but the movement continued. The BTR accord was signed in January 2020 with ABSU and four NDFB factions.

The BTC administers the four districts of Kokrajhar, Chirang, Baksa and Udalguri, falling under the BTR.

CHAPTER III

Role of All India Bodo People's National League for Bodoland Statehood (AIBPNLBS)

The All India Bodo People's National League for Bodoland Statehood (AIBPNLBS), under the special initiative of former MP SK Bwiswmuthiary, was formed to re-launch the Bodoland movement in the second special convention of former All Bodo Students' Union (ABSU) leaders, workers, supporters, intellectuals and leaders of Boro civil society organizations held on 15 October 2020 at Neervana Garden, Kokrajhar.

An ad-hoc committee of nine members was also formed and headed by Sansuma Khungur Bwiswmuthiary as President, Gajen Hazoary, Sukracharjya Muchahary and Dr. Phukhan Chandra Boro as Vice-Presidents, Jebra Ram Muchahary, Nitya Nanda Basumatary and Daorao Dekreb Narzary as General Secretary, Joint Secretary and Chief Convener respectively. Hiracharan Narzinary and Janaklal Basumatary were selected as Advisors of AIBPNLBS.

Talking to reporters, Bwiswmuthiary said that the third Bodo accord signed on January 27, 2020 brought the concept of the misnomer 'Bodoland Territory Region'. He said that the detrimental political move of the State Government to grant ST status to the undeserving six communities by way of recommending to the Centre through the committee of the group of ministers headed by Dr. Himanta Biswa Sarma was aimed to exterminate all the aboriginal tribal people of Assam in totality. He also said that the State Government's humiliating policy decision to notify the most ancient and rich Bodo language as a mere associate official language of Assam was an ulterior design to deprive the Bodo language of getting the status of State official language. Bwiswmuthiary said the AIBPNLBS would demand for holding the general election to BTC within the month of October 2020. Organized by the Convener Committee, former ABSU leaders, members, workers, supporters and well-wishers and intellectuals participated in day-long programme.

CHAPTER IV

Conclusion

The major phases, waves and generations of the Bodoland Movement ended with the signing of the historic Bodo Accord on 27th January 2020.

But the movement for a separate state Bodoland still awaits a final resolution.

References

^ "(T)he Bodo leadership in 1967 formed a political party called the Plains Tribals Council of Assam (PTCA). Since its formation, the PTCA has categorically demanded a union territory for the Bodosand other Plains tribals of the region called Udayachal." (George 1994:879)

^ "When Biswa Singha (1515-40) rose to power, the local chiefs, who ruled the country between the river Sonkosh and the Baradi were subdued and the Koch occupied the Duar areas." (Das 1998:29)

^ "[Nara Narayana] further instructed the Meches and Koches living to the north of the Gosain Kamal Ali to follow their tribal customs, but in the territory south of this road as far as the Brahmaputra Brahmanic rites were to be continued." (Nath 1989:55)

^ Naranarayan placed an image of Goddess Durga and appointed a Kachari as its priest. He then collected all the Bhutias of Duars, the Kacharis and Meches living between the Bhutan hills and the Gohain Kamal Ali and ordered that the former could follow their tribal custom in the territory upto the Gohain Kamal Ali.(Das 1998:31–32)

^ "Taking advantage of [the collapse of Koch Hajo], the Bhutias pushed their southern boundary towards the plains and occupied the land upto the Gohain Kamal Ali." (Das 1998:13)

^ "During the period of political uncertainty caused by the Ahom-Mughal conflict in the middle of seventeenth century, the Bhutias had taken possession of the whole of the fertile plain south of their hills as far as the Gohain Kamal Ali." (Das 1998:59)

REFERENCES

^ "These Duars play crucial role in the determination of the relations between Assam and Bhutan. The term 'Duar' literally meaning 'door' in English, is used to refer to the areas below the foothills is equivalent to Bhutanese 'las-sgo' (lit. work-door) which always carries the sense of a border mart at the foot of a pass and the area in its immediate vicinity." (Das 1998:26)

Bibliography

Allen, B.C (1905). Assam District Gazetteers-kamrup Vol. 4. The Pioneer Press, Allahabad.

Brahma, Nirjay Kumar (2008). "Introduction: Interpretation of Bodo or Boro". Socio political institutions in Bodo society (PhD). Gauhati University. hdl:10603/66535.

Das, Smriti (1998). Assam Bhutan relations with special reference to duars from 1681 to 1949 (PhD). Guwahati University. hdl:10603/67909.

Deka, Hira Moni (2009). "The Historical Background of Bodo Movement". Politics of identity and the bodo movement in Assam (PhD). Gauhati University. hdl:10603/67844.

George, Sudhir Jacob (1994). "The Bodo Movement in Assam: Unrest to Accord". Asian Survey. 34 (10): 878–892. doi:10.2307/2644967. JSTOR 2644967.

Nath, D. (1989). History of the Koch Kingdom, C. 1515-1615. Mittal Publications. ISBN 8170991099.

Roy, Ajoy (1995). The Bodo Imbroglio. Spectrum Publications. ISBN 8185319588.

Dikshit, K. R.; Dikshit, Jutta K. (2013). North-East India: Land, People and Economy. Springer Science & Business Media. pp. 375–376. ISBN 978-94-007-7055-3.

Phuntsho, Karma (2013). The History of Bhutan. Penguin Books. ISBN 9781908323583.

Phukan, J N (2014). "Ahom-Bhutan Relations with Specific Reference to Royal Bhutanese Embassy Visiting Ahom Capital in 1801" (PDF). Journal of Bhutan Studies. 30 (Summer 2014).